Mapping the Seas

Mapping the Seas

Walter Oleksy

Watts LIBRARY™

Franklin Watts
A Division of Scholastic Inc.
New York • Toronto • London • Auckland • Sydney
Mexico City • New Delhi • Hong Kong
Danbury, Connecticut

Note to readers: Definitions for words in **bold** can be found in the Glossary at the back of this book.

Photographs © 2002: Art Resource, NY/Giraudon: 12; Bridgeman Art Library International Ltd., London/New York: cover (British Library, London, UK), 16, 17, 20, 21 (Private Collection), 26 (Royal Geographical Society, London); Corbis Images: 25 (Austrian Archives), 28, 32 (Bettmann), 2 (Jacques M. Chenet), 14, 15 (Gianni Dagli Orti), 18 (MAPS.com), 44 (Ralph White), 5 left, 30, 39 bottom, 39 top; NOAA Central Library: 41 (C&GS Season's Report Edmonston), 5 right, 23, 31, 34; Photo Researchers, NY: 11 (Los Alamos National Laboratory/SPL), 47 (NASA/SPL), 9 (Tom Van Sant/Geosphere Project, Santa Monica/SPL); Superstock, Inc./The Huntington Library, Art Collections and Botanical Gardens, San Marino, California: 22, 24; UNEP-WCMC: 42; Visuals Unlimited: 45 (John S. Lough), 6 (NOAA); Woods Hole Oceanographic Institution: 33 (Rod Catanach), 37.

The photograph on the cover shows a map of Arabia and the East Mediterranean Sea. The photograph opposite the title page shows U.S. Coast Guard personnel studying a chart.

Library of Congress Cataloging-in-Publication Data

Oleksy, Walter G., 1930–
 Mapping the seas / by Walter Oleksy.
  p. cm. — (Watts library)
 Includes bibliographical references and index.
 ISBN 0-531-12030-9 (lib. bdg.) 0-531-16634-1 (pbk.)
 1. Ocean—Maps for children. Oceanography—Charts, diagrams, etc.—Juvenile literature.
[1. Ocean—Maps. 2. Oceanography—Charts, diagrams, etc.] I. Title. II. Series.
GA359 .O54 2002
551.46'0022'3—dc21

2001004940

Contents

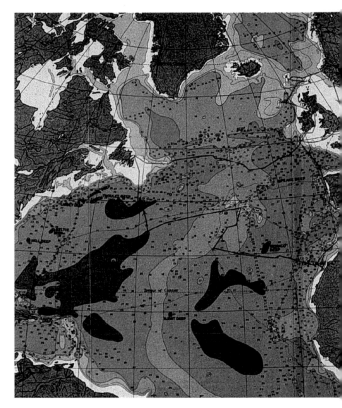

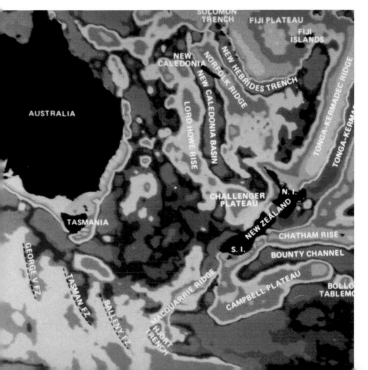

From this image of the world, it is easy to see how much of our planet is water.

Chapter One

Origins of Sea Mapping

From space, planet Earth looks mostly blue, the predominant color of the oceans and seas seen from a great distance. Actually, many bodies of water look green because of the algae and plant life in them. Oceans are vast open bodies of water separating **continents** from each other. Seas are large bodies of saltwater, but they are smaller than oceans and partly, or entirely, enclosed by land. A sea may also be part of an ocean, such as the Sargasso Sea in the North Atlantic

Ocean. Often, the words *sea* and *ocean* are used to mean the same thing.

Earth's oceans and seas originated about 4.5 billion years ago. They cover almost 71 percent—or about two-thirds—of the planet's surface. Because they are so vast and deep, only a small percent of Earth's waters have been mapped.

Earth's five largest bodies of water are really one huge connected ocean, with many branches that are given individual names. The Pacific Ocean lies between the west coasts of North and South America and the east coasts of Asia, the Malay archipelago, and Australia. It is bordered on the north by the Bering Strait and on the south by Antarctica. The largest ocean, it is about 64 million square miles (166 million square kilometers) in area. It also is the deepest ocean, about 36,198 feet (11,033 meters) at the Mariana **Trench** off Guam in the Northwest Pacific.

The Atlantic Ocean lies between the east coasts of North and South America and the west coasts of Europe and Africa. It extends from the Arctic Ocean in the north to the Anarctic continent in the south. It is the second largest ocean, about 32 million square miles (82 million sq km) in area. It is 28,231 feet (8,605 m) deep at the Puerto Rico Trench.

The Indian Ocean lies between the east coast of Africa and the west coast of Australia. It runs north to Asia and south to Antarctica. It is 28 million square miles (73 million sq km) in area and its maximum depth is 25,344 feet (7,725 m). The Arctic Ocean at the top of the world is 5.4 million square miles

How the Great Oceans Were Named

The Atlantic Ocean's name was derived from Atlas, one of the Titans of Greek mythology. The Pacific Ocean was named in 1520 by Portuguese **navigator** Ferdinand Magellan on his voyage around the world. After sailing through storms in the Atlantic, his ship encountered days of calm weather in the Pacific, so he named it *Mar Pacifico*, "peaceful ocean."

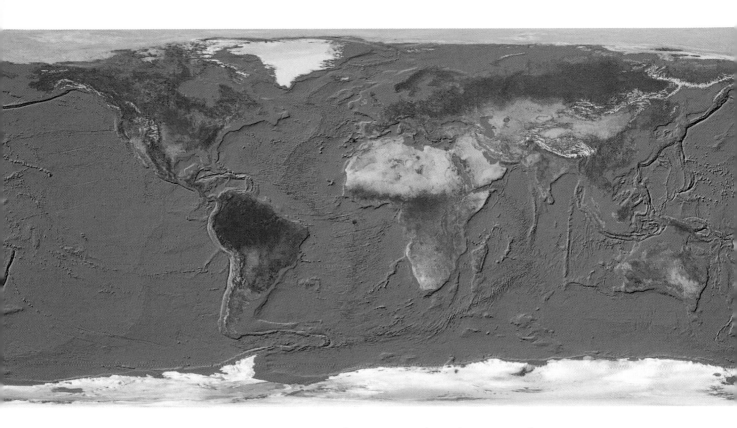

(13.9 million sq km) in area, most of it covered with ice, and its maximum depth 17,880 feet (5,450 m). The Antarctic Ocean at the bottom of the world is 11 million square miles (28 million km) in area, and the maximum depth of the Antarctic ice sheet is 15,400 feet (4,700 m).

The Earth has about seventy seas. The South China Sea is the largest sea at 895,400 square miles (2,319,000 sq km) in area, and 15,000 feet (4,600 m) in maximum depth. Other major seas include the Mediterranean Sea, Caribbean Sea, North Sea, Red Sea, Dead Sea (the saltiest sea in the world), Black Sea, Adriatic Sea, and Caspian Sea. They also include smaller seas, such as the Gulf of Mexico and the Persian Gulf.

This computer-generated picture shows the world's oceans.

How Some Major Seas Got Their Names

The Mediterranean Sea's name is derived from the Latin words *medius*, which means "middle" and *terra*, which means "earth." *Mediterranean* means "the sea in the middle of the earth," which ancient sailors believed it was.

The Caribbean Sea is named after the Carib people of the Central and South American coast. They were said to be cannibals—eaters of human flesh. Sailors feared landing on their islands. The Black Sea was named by ancient Turks because they were terrified of its vast open waters and storms. The Dead Sea, actually a salt lake, was named by Romans because its extremely salty waters support almost no life.

Why Map the Seas?

Life on Earth could not survive without the seas and oceans. They control our planet's climate, although scientists still do not really understand how. It is known that they play a major role in the balance of nature between Earth's land, waters, and air that affects weather.

The seas are home to millions of different plants and animals including about twenty thousand species of fishes. They provide food for millions of people all over the world. Seas and oceans also act like giant heaters, spreading the Sun's warmth around the world.

Seas and oceans are vast reservoirs of water that recycle rain, preventing continents from turning into deserts. The enormous stores of oil, gas, and minerals under the ocean floors help to fuel the modern world. Knowing how the seas function, what they contain, and where their various vast

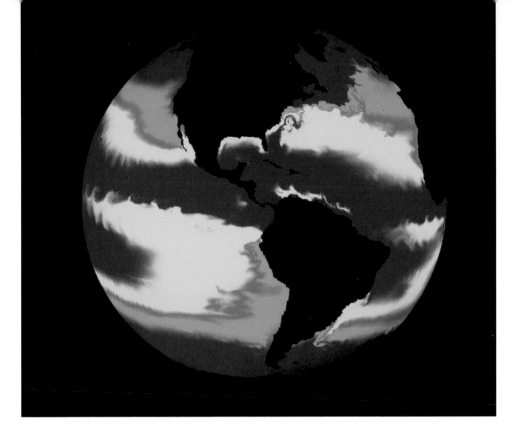

This computerized model shows the temperatures of the ocean surface. The red areas are the warmest and the blue areas are the coldest.

wealth is located are some additional reasons why mapping the seas and oceans is of vital importance.

The First Voyagers

Mapping the seas began before recorded time when sailors and scientists wondered what land lay beyond the watery horizon they could see with their eyes. Over the centuries, this

Daring Sea Voyages

South American sailors in ancient times may have built small sailing rafts to reach islands in the far western Pacific. Norwegian explorer Thor Heyerdahl proved such a journey was possible by rigging a sail to a reed raft and making a similar voyage in 1947.

curiosity led to voyages of exploration that resulted in maps of the coastlines of land surfaces such as the continents. Discovering what lay beneath the surface of the seas and oceans mainly became a pursuit of scientists over the past two hundred years.

Ancient sailors were both fascinated and fearful of the open seas and oceans. They rowed or sailed their boats or ships close to the safe and familiar shore, afraid to venture into the

This carving shows a Phoenician ship from around A.D. 100.

distant watery unknown. Even brave Phoenicians who sailed throughout the Mediterranean Sea on voyages of trade around 1500 B.C. also seldom sailed beyond the sight of land.

Coastal landmarks guided Phoenician sailors living where Syria and Lebanon are today. They began recording landmarks on sea charts, or maps, in about 3000 B.C. Mountains, islands, harbors, and other natural landmarks guided them from port to port. Inlets—narrow passages between islands—were noted on sea charts, as were bays—portions of ocean enclosed partly by land. Phoenician sailors circumnavigated Africa from east to west following sea charts in 700 B.C.

Early mapping of the Atlantic Ocean may have begun when the Greek explorer Pytheas sailed north to England and the North Sea in 330 B.C. The North Atlantic Ocean was later explored by the Vikings who reached Iceland by A.D. 800s, Greenland by the late 900s, and the North American coast in about 1000. No Viking maps survive, however.

In A.D. 150, Claudius Ptolemy, a Greek **astronomer**, drew a map of the world showing it to be round, not flat. He published a set of books called *Geography*, which listed the latitude and longitude of eight thousand places. His work became the

Sea Monsters

Sailors as late as the 1700s feared the sea monsters that they thought inhabited the seas and oceans. They may have mistaken huge whales, sharks, and octopuses, which do live in the seas, for monsters.

The First Sea Charts

Around the second century A.D., a Greek, Marinus of Tyre, made the first sea charts, maps sailors used for navigation that included lines of **latitude** and **longitude**. Latitude is the distance north or south of the **equator**. Longitude is the distance east and west.

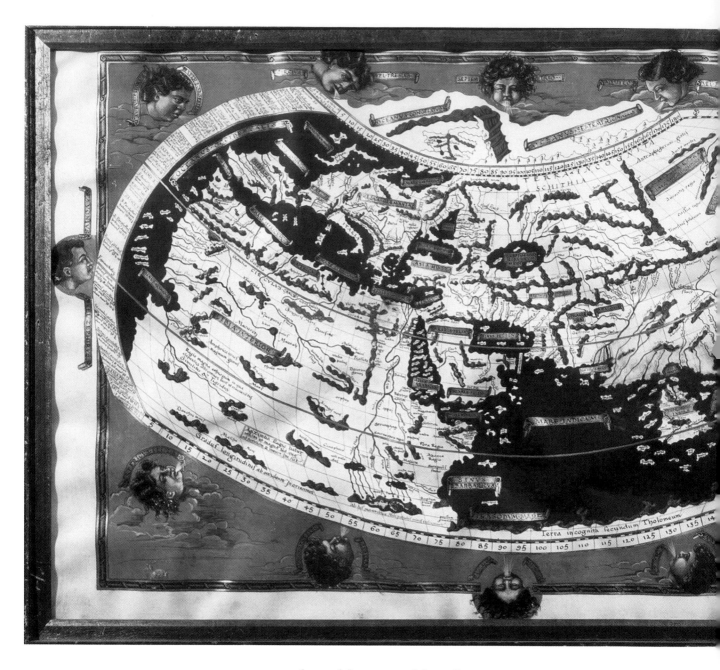

This map of the world is based on the work of Ptolemy.

cornerstone of world mapmaking for centuries. Later, inaccuracies in Ptolemy's work, such as the true **circumference** of the world, were discovered. He underestimated the distance

around the world by approximately one-third.

Early mapping of the Pacific Ocean began when Polynesians began colonizing the major island groups by about A.D. 400. Chinese and Japanese sailors charted the seas close to their shores as well as in the South China Sea and Indian Ocean, although no charts have survived. By the end of the 1400s, the Chinese had mapped in detail vast parts of Southeast Asia, the east coast of India, and parts of the Philippines.

Stick and Shell Maps

Micronesian sailors in the western Pacific Ocean in ancient times devised a simple way to chart parts of the ocean. Curved sticks stood for ocean swells, and shells represented islands.

The three ships of Columbus sail toward the East Indies, one of the many expeditions during the Age of Discovery.

Chapter Two

Navigating the Seas

From the 1400s to the late 1700s, kings and queens of England, Spain, Portugal, France, and the Netherlands sent ships across the Atlantic and Pacific Oceans in search of new territories upon which to place their flag. The importance of the Age of Exploration to mapping is that it led to greater knowledge of where distant islands and continents lay on the seas and oceans, and how far the sailors were from home ports. On their voyages, sailors also learned more about the physical dangers

Finding Your Way

Navigation is the science of finding out where you are on Earth's surface, and then being able to find your way from there to anywhere else you want to go.

This map shows the voyage of Magellan's expedition.

of sailing the seas. These included fierce storms that might sink ships, and **currents**, rivers flowing through the surface waters of all major oceans, capable of taking their ship off course.

The Age of Exploration began in 1418 when Prince Henry the Navigator of Portugal founded a school for the study of navigation and other **oceanographic** information. Fifty Portuguese naval expeditions then explored the world. The first voyage was made to the west coast of Africa to find a new sea route to the spice-rich lands of India and Southeast Asia.

Over the next three hundred years, European navigators explored the world. Christopher Columbus, Bartholomew Dias, and Vasco da Gama sailed the Atlantic Ocean. Explorers

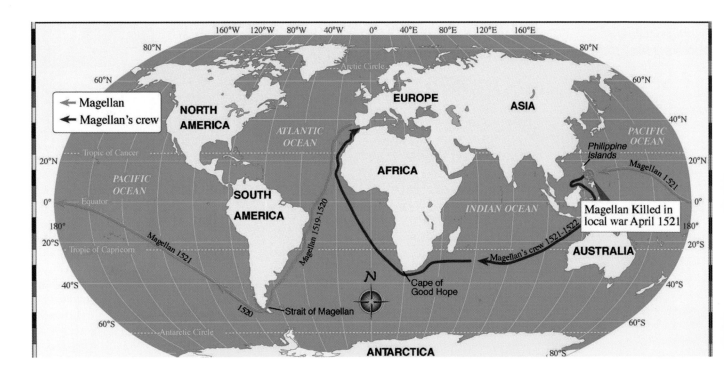

of the Pacific Ocean included Vasco Núñez de Balboa, Juan Ponce de León, and James Cook. In 1519, Ferdinand Magellan led a Spanish expedition that **circumnavigated** the world and proved it to be round. The voyages produced a wealth of new information for mapmakers.

Modern mapmaking probably began around 1507 when Martin Waldseemüller, a German geographer and **cartographer**, published his *World Sea Maps*. The name *America* was first used on his maps. He published an even more comprehensive set of world maps in 1516, which were widely copied by other mapmakers and used by navigators. A copy of each of his maps, the only ones known to exist today, were found in a German castle in 1901.

Because of all these voyages, the North Atlantic Ocean was fairly well explored and mapped by the early 1500s. Mapping of the South Atlantic took longer. One important step took place in 1520, when Ferdinand Magellan sailed around Tierra del Fuego at the tip of South America. This voyage proved it was a group of islands and not part of a southern continent.

Mapping of the Pacific Ocean, so far as its major land locations go, was completed at the end of the 1500s. This was

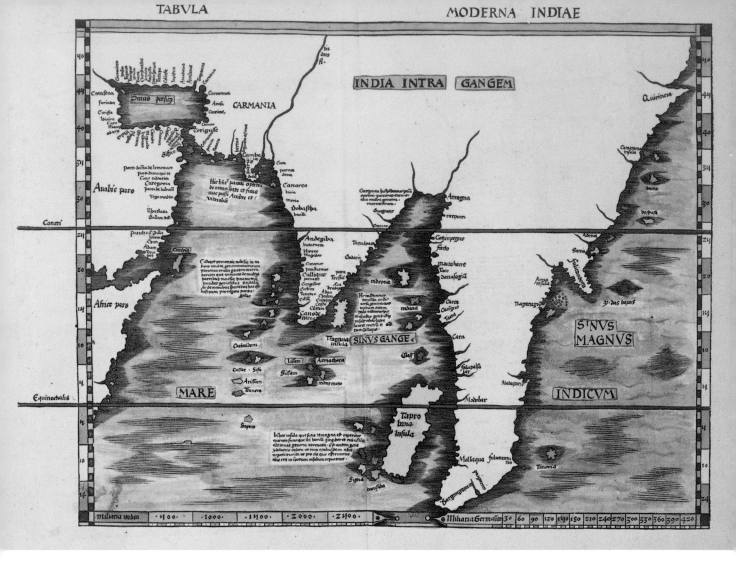

Martin Waldseemüller created this map, which shows the Red Sea and the Arabian Gulf.

shown on a 1601 Spanish map by Antonio de Herera. It included the southeastern coast of China, Japan, Borneo, the Philippines, and New Guinea.

Early Scientific Mappers

The first organized attempt to study the oceans and seas occurred during the Atlantic and Pacific Ocean voyages of

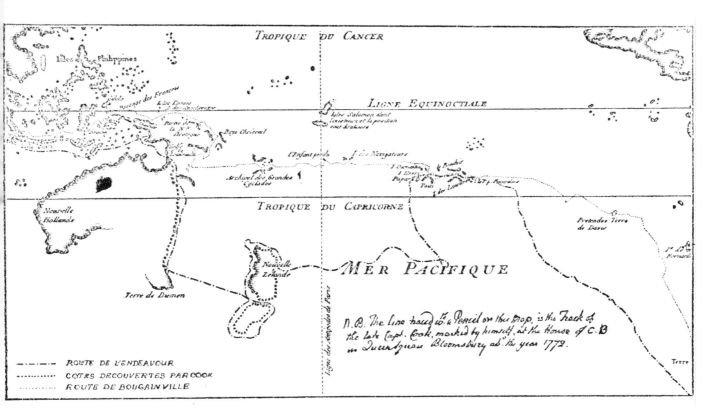

Within the map:

TROPIQUE DU CANCER

Isles de Philippines

LIGNE EQUINOCTIALE

Isles Salomon dont l'existence et la position sont douteuses

TROPIQUE DU CAPRICORNE

MER PACIFIQUE

Nouvelle Zelande

Terre de Diemen

N.B. The line traced in a Pencil on this map, is the Track of the late Capt. Cook, marked by himself, at the House of C. B in Queen Square Bloomsbury abt. the year 1772.

ROUTE DE L'ENDEAVOUR
COTES DECOUVERTES PAR COOK
ROUTE DE BOUGAINVILLE

This French map shows the routes taken by James Cook and Louis Antoine de Bougainville around the world.

British Captain James Cook, who discovered Hawaii, from 1768 to 1779. An excellent mapmaker and chart maker, Cook mapped coasts and islands that clarified the main outline of the Pacific. Later explorers had only to fill in the details.

Cook took with him a natural historian and two astronomers who conducted scientific studies such as recording subsurface temperatures and taking **soundings**, or depth readings, of the oceans. Soundings were taken by lowering a weighted rope over the side of a ship to the seafloor. Marks on the rope told the person taking the soundings the distance to the seafloor. Today, soundings are made by **sonar**, instruments

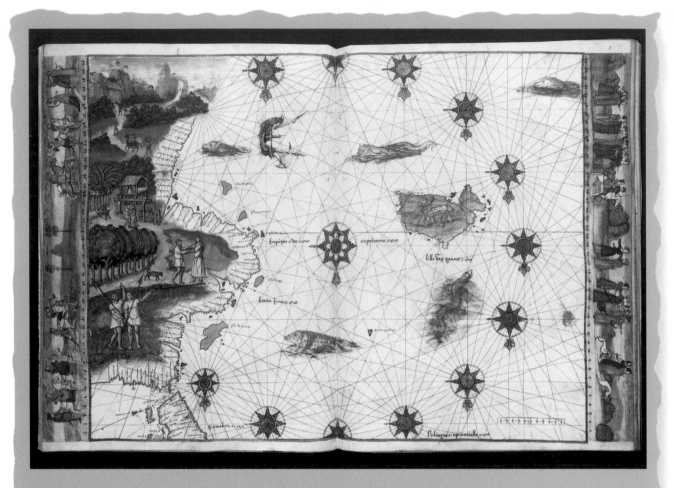

Maps as Art

Early hand-drawn maps were often works of art. Mapmakers drew paintings of imaginary sea monsters in the ocean sections of maps, or seashells and other decorative objects from the oceans, along their borders. Artists have often painted the dangers of sea travel, such as the Japanese artist Hokusai whose painting, *The Breaking Wave off Kanagawa*, depicts a small boat being engulfed by a stormswept sea. Many of American artist Winslow Homer's paintings are of the angry sea, such as *The Gulf Stream* showing a lone sailor in a small boat threatened by sharks. The Gulf Stream is part of a system of warm ocean currents that flow northward in the North Atlantic Ocean. Homer excelled in watercolors of the sea, which are now displayed in many museums.

that send down pulses of sound and record the distance the echo has traveled.

Inspired by the Cook expeditions, Alexander Von Humboldt, a German scientist, made a major contribution to ocean mapping in 1802 by discovering a current in the southeastern Pacific Ocean. Taking measurements of the 500-mile (800-km) wide cold-water flow of the ocean, he learned that it greatly affects weather at times. It later became known as the Humboldt Current.

American inventor, author, and statesman Benjamin Franklin also contributed scientific knowledge about the oceans. In 1770 he published his findings from an Atlantic Ocean voyage during which he became the first person to plot the course of the Gulf Stream and draw a map of it. He suggested that captains could increase their ship's speed by taking advantage of what he called the North Atlantic Current when sailing east, and avoiding it when sailing west.

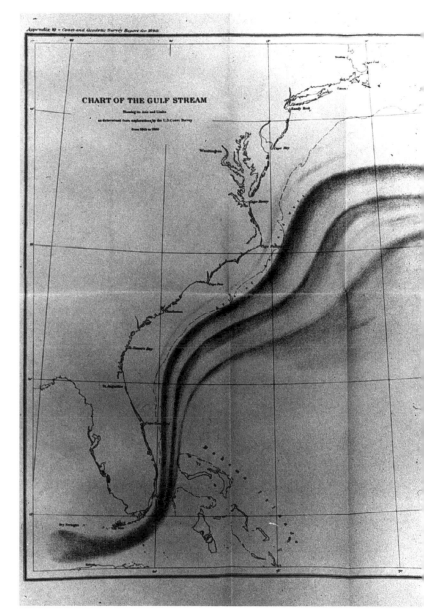

This map of the Gulf Stream was based on a series of studies done by the Coast Survey in the mid-1800s.

Charting the Course

The first European sea charts were called **portolan charts**—port or harbor-finding charts—used by those sailing the Mediterranean Sea at the end of the 1200s. The main feature of portolan charts was the network of course directions, lines already drawn on the charts, with **compass** bearings written on them, that connected the most commonly used ports. A compass is a navigational instrument for finding direction by showing where north is. Portolans were usually drawn on sheepskin or goatskin. They showed natural features such as harbors and coastlines, but no details of what lay inland.

Sailors used the red lines on portolan charts to help them get to where they wanted to go.

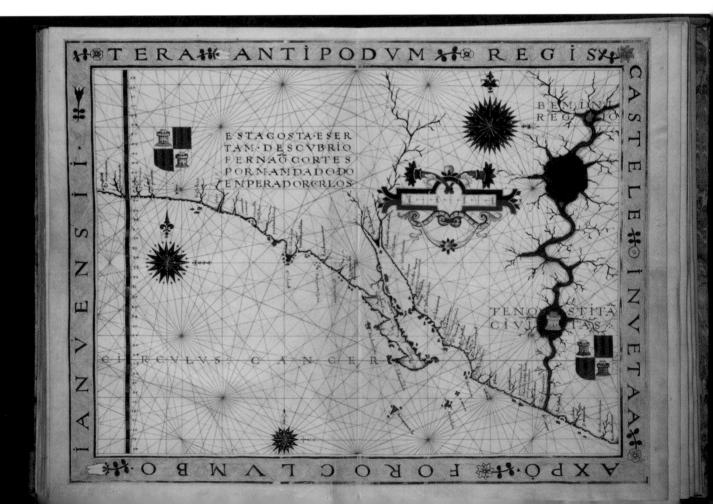

Besides maps, sailors relied on a number of tools to help them find their way. The place and date of invention of the compass are unknown, but the Chinese used that instrument to sail to East Africa in the 700s. The compass first appeared in European literature in the 1100s. A mariner's magnetic compass, developed by the late 1200s, resembles today's Boy Scout or Girl Scout compass. It consists of a magnetic needle freely suspended so that, in the Earth's magnetic field, it turns to align itself with the magnetic north pole.

The compass alone, however, did not help navigators determine the location of their ship at sea, or find a distant place. An accurate map was needed. But the only type of map that is completely accurate is a global or round map because the Earth is round. The Greek astronomer and geographer Ptolemy represented a round **globe** on a flat map by a system called projection, in the 100s.

It was not until 1569 that a more accurate way of showing the globe on a flat piece of paper was found. Gerardus Mercator, a Flemish geographer, devised a system of map projection

The Astrolabe

Greek sailors used an astrolabe for navigation in the 100s B.C. The astrolabe was a round instrument used to determine latitude by measuring the angles—the height above the horizon—of the Sun, Moon, planets, and stars. Using mathematical tables and formulas, the sailors could figure out the latitude of the place where the measurement was taken.

Mercator created this map of Europe using his projection system.

using lines of latitude and longitude to help navigators plot more accurate maps. Mariners used the Mercator projection map to plot a straight-line course across long distances without changing direction.

In order to find a place while sailing, such as a harbor or an island, it is essential to know its latitude and longitude.

Latitude is the measurement of distance north or south of the equator. It could be measured with some accuracy by the 1500s. Longitude is the measurement of distance east and west of a location. Longitude, which is measured in minutes and relies on accurate time-keeping, would not be precisely measured for another two hundred years, however. Shipboard clocks before then did not keep accurate time because of a vessel's movements on the seas.

The problem of determining precise longitude was solved when the marine **chronometer**, a timekeeper with a special mechanism for ensuring accuracy, was invented in the 1760s by British instrument maker John Harrison. It revolutionized both navigation and mapmaking because locations of landforms could be accurately placed on a sea chart and reached by ship. As a result, charts became more uniform and universally used.

The Sextant

Invented about 1730, the sextant is an optical instrument used for measuring the angle of the Sun, Moon, a planet, or a star above the horizon. The sextant is mainly used for navigation at sea. By knowing the angle of the heavenly body above the horizon, sailors could calculate the latitude.

Besides exploring the Pacific Ocean, Charles Wilkes also ventured to the coastal areas of Antarctica. Part of Antarctica bears his name—it is called Wilkes Land.

Chapter Three

Mapping the Depths

General mapping of the seas and oceans—noting where the major land-masses are located—was virtually completed by the end of the 1500s. Scientific mapping of their surfaces and depths began after the mid-1700s and continues to this day. A major step forward in this pursuit was called the Great U.S. Exploring Expedition, which mapped the Pacific Ocean from 1838 to 1842.

Approved by Congress and directed by the U.S. Navy, the expedition's

Wilkes helped create this map of Oregon.

purpose was to gather scientific data about the ocean. The expedition also was designed to enable the United States to make territorial claims on its islands. Commanding the expedition was Charles Wilkes, a young officer with scientific and **surveying** abilities.

While nine civilian scientists and artists on the expedition gathered and took notes on 160,000 specimens of plant and animal life in the Pacific, Wilkes trained them in drawing maps. The result was two **atlases** with 241 maps of the northwest coast of North America, the Columbia River, the Antarctic Ocean, and 280 islands in the Pacific Ocean. The maps were so complete and accurate that they were used by United States and British forces during World War II (1939–1945).

The *Challenger* Expedition

The first major expedition to map the ocean depths was the round-the-world British *Challenger* Expedition of 1872–1876, commanded by Charles Wyville Thomson. Five scientists aboard the British sailing ship H.M.S. *Challenger* took hundreds of depth soundings, and studied currents and ocean temperatures. Some 4,400 newly discovered species of marine life were safely stored in water-filled bottles for later study. Findings from the historic expedition—more than had been learned in all previous voyages in history—filled fifty volumes. They provided the groundwork for every major branch of modern **oceanography**.

A most significant achievement of the *Challenger* Expedition was discovering the Mid-Atlantic Ridge, a submerged mountain range that runs down the middle of the ocean. It is both the longest and tallest mountain range on Earth. Mountains under the oceans and seas were formed by volcanoes on the seabed. The Mid-Atlantic Ridge is 300 to 600 miles (480 to 970 km) wide, extends 10,000 miles (16,100 km) from Iceland to near the Antarctic, and rises to an average height of 10,000 feet (3,048 m).

This map shows the bottom temperature of the Atlantic Ocean. The Mid-Atlantic Ridge obstructs the cool water in the southwest Atlantic from reaching the southeast.

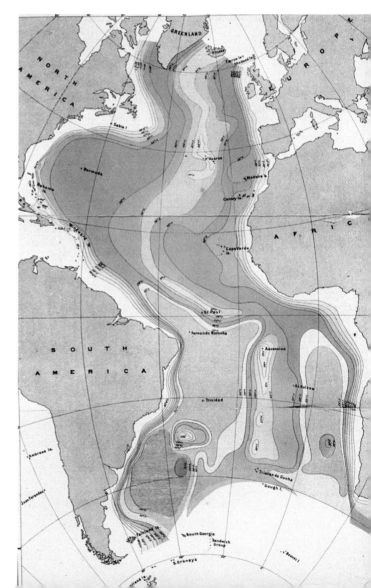

Challenger's depth soundings also led to discovery of the first of Earth's ocean trenches—the long, narrow V-shaped valleys in the deepest parts of the seabed. The Mariana Trench, more than 36,000 feet (11,000 m) deep, was found near Guam when sounding lines ran out after extending more than five miles down into the Pacific Ocean. Pitch black and freezing cold, most ocean trenches lie 6,561 to 13,123 feet (2,000 to 4,000 m) below the rest of the seafloor.

Diving, Submersibles, and Submarines

The **diving bell** was invented by British astronomer Edmund Halley in 1690, and it enabled divers to work on the seafloor. First, air was pumped into the bell, a wooden chamber large enough for a person to stand. The air was then sent through a tube to a diver wearing a hood to receive the air and breathe while walking on the seabed.

By the 1800s, divers wore waterproof rubberized suits with attached screw-on copper helmets to which air was pumped through hoses on shipboard. SCUBA—Self-Contained Underwater Breathing Apparatus—was invented by French scientists Jacques Cousteau and Émile Gagnan in 1943. This device gave divers freedom to swim with their own air supply, which comes from cylinders strapped to their back.

A **submersible** is smaller than a submarine. It travels under the ocean for research or to recover sunken objects. The first submersible was a cast-iron sphere called a

This illustration shows the inside of the diving bell.

bathysphere. The bathysphere held two divers and was built in the 1930s by Otis Barton and William Beebe. More modern submersibles appeared in the 1960s. Today they can dive to about 21,320 feet (6,500 m). The most modern submersible today is the *Alvin*, operated by Woods Hole Oceanographic Institution and launched in 1964.

Submarines can spend months at sea without surfacing. The first submarine that could remain underwater for six hours was invented in 1802 by Robert Fulton, the inventor of the steamboat. In 1897, Simon Lake's *Argonaut* became the first submarine to navigate in the open sea.

Gasoline-powered submarines first crossed the Atlantic Ocean in 1912. The United States *Nautilus*, the first nuclear-powered submarine, became the first ship to sail beneath the ice at the North Pole, in 1955. Two years later, another United States nuclear-powered submarine, the *Triton*, sailed around the world underwater.

Deep Submergence Vehicle Alvin *is lowered into the ocean. A typical dive lasts six to ten hours.*

Heezen and Tharp
helped advance our
knowledge of the
Atlantic Ocean through
their scientific research.

Chapter Four

Modern Ocean Mapping

Modern research of the oceans began in 1947 when two American **oceanographers** from Columbia University, Bruce Heezen and Marie Tharp, carried on the work of the *Challenger* expedition of 1873–1876 by further exploring the depths of the Atlantic Ocean. Taking soundings from a ship above the Mid-Atlantic Ridge, Heezen and Tharp made the first accurate maps of that vast mountain range.

Deep-sea photographs taken with an

International Geophysical Year

Worldwide cooperation in studying and mapping Earth's oceans, glaciers, upper atmosphere, geology, and weather was achieved in the International Geophysical Year (IGY), actually two and a half years, from 1957 to 1959. Scientists from seventy countries took part in the research effort. Maps were involved in every step of the process, from planning projects to finding sites for research stations to communicating the data gathered by researchers.

Many projects concerned mapping. Observers in many stations made new determinations of latitude and longitude so that existing maps could be corrected and new ones prepared. Airplanes, balloons, and rockets were used to take pictures that helped cartographers refine their maps. The IGY paved the way for international cooperation on many scientific projects involving the seas and oceans, including many mapping projects that continue today.

automatic camera developed by Maurice Ewing, also of Columbia University, provided close-up views of the ocean floor. The photos provided evidence to support a geologic theory known as continental drift. The term applies to the theory that thousands of years ago the continents were joined as one supercontinent called Pangaea. It had eventually broken apart and the pieces, called plates, had drifted to the present positions of the continents. The theory was first proposed by the German scientist Alfred Wegener in 1915.

No one knew how these events happened until oceanic exploration such as that of Heezen and Tharp in the 1950s led to evidence that seafloor spreading caused the continents to drift apart. Their photos showed that the continents rest on top of large, slow-moving plates of the Earth's crust. They also revealed how ridges and rifts in the ocean floor mark places where the plates met or moved apart.

What causes the ocean floor to spread is still a mystery. However, it is known that the Atlantic Ocean is growing, while the Pacific Ocean shrinks as the American continental plates override its eastern rim. Such continental drift could have profound effects on the planet. It could produce earthquakes of major proportions. Ocean water levels could rise and engulf coastal cities as well–this also could happen if the polar ice caps melt faster than is anticipated.

In 1973 and 1974, scientists with Project FAMOUS (French-American Mid-Ocean Undersea Study) became the first to actually view the mid-Atlantic seafloor. They made forty-seven dives in three submersibles to become the first humans to reach the floor of the Atlantic rift valley. Such close-up examination of the ocean floors can provide maps that may answer the mystery of what is causing the ocean floor to move.

This computer-generation illustration shows the seafloor of part of the Mid-Atlantic Ridge.

Satellite Sea Mapping

Satellites are objects placed in **orbit** around the Earth that collect information and transmit it back to Earth. They carry cameras and remote-sensing equipment that see below the surface of the oceans and send the information back to Earth by radio signals. Remote sensing is the process of examining something without touching it or approaching it directly. This technology is providing even more detail for mapping the ocean depths without humans actually being on the ocean floor.

In 1978, the American Seasat satellite measured the ocean's floor using **microwaves** to record variations in the level of the sea's surface. Microwaves are **electromagnetic waves** of extremely high frequency. Cartographer William Haxby used the data to make the most detailed map yet of the ocean floor. It showed hundreds of previously unknown sea mountains.

The Geosat satellite, launched in 1985, yielded extensive and detailed information about the structure of the ocean floor. Haxby used the new data to make three-dimensional computer-generated maps of parts of the oceans. Satellites, such as Geosat, ERS-1, and ERS-2, continue to provide new information about the oceans. They monitor sea level, wave height and direction, surface temperatures, wind speeds, currents, sea ice, and levels of marine plant life. Many scientists believe that the combination of satellites and maps provides a priceless tool for preserving and protecting Earth's environment.

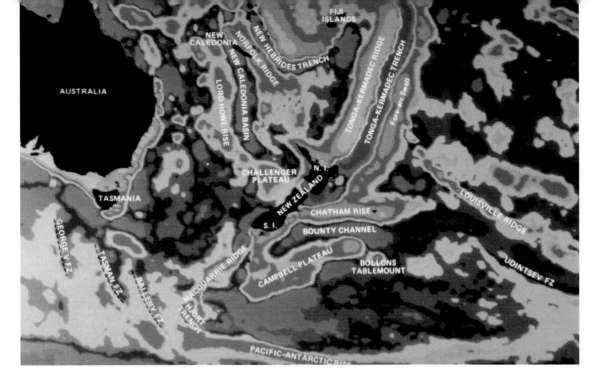

With data received from the Seasat satellite, cartographers made this map of the southwestern Pacific (above).

This map of wave height (below) was created with information from the Ocean Topography Experiment satellite, or TOPEX.

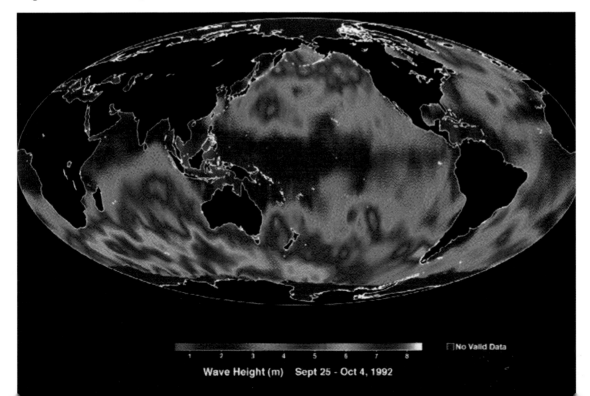

Wave Height (m)   Sept 25 - Oct 4, 1992

No Valid Data

Maps in Wartime

Maps are of vital importance in wartime, to know where an enemy's armies and fortifications were on land, or to find the ports their ships might be in at sea. Much was learned of the waters, islands, and mainlands of the Aegean Sea in the wars between Persia and the Greek colonies in the late 400s B.C. Similarly, mapmaking was a part of the strategy used in the Peloponnesian Wars, which began in 431 B.C. among the Greek city states in the Aegean.

Maps became necessities for war strategy over the following centuries, including the American Civil War (1861–1865). Mapmakers in both the Union and Confederate armies produced maps showing enemy locations, while Union Navy mapmakers served with the blockading squadrons off Charleston, South Carolina, and on the Mississippi River. During World War I (1914–1918), not only generals but field soldiers relied on maps to locate enemy positions. At sea, maps and new oceanic **acoustic**—audio or sound—research helped to detect locations of enemy submarines.

New maps of Europe contributed greatly to the defeat of the Nazis in Europe and Africa and of the Japanese in the Pacific during World War II (1939–1945). Naval and air campaigns were planned from detailed maps of the seas, islands, and mainlands of the Pacific. Two important new mapping technologies—**radar** and sonar—became widely used during that war. Radar is a detecting device that utilizes radio waves. Sonar instruments locate positions of objects by emitting sounds and timing the echoes that bounce back. The importance of war mapping continues today, as satellite **surveillance** mapping has been used in Afghanistan and other countries in the war against terrorism.

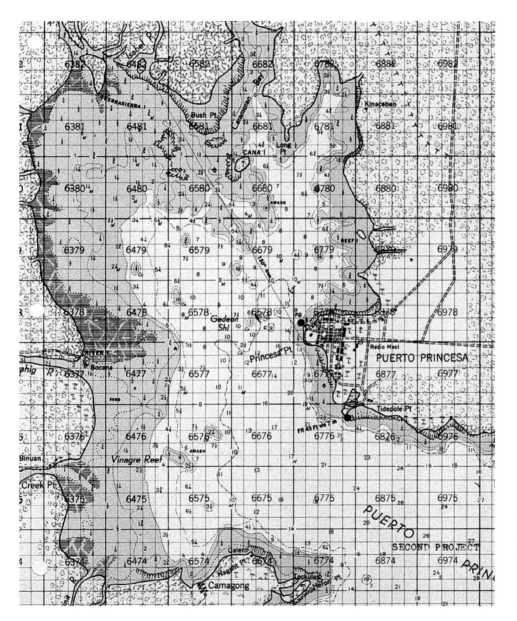

This is a map of a part of the Philippines. This chart helped U.S. forces determine the best routes to transport soldiers and equipment during World War II.

Today, computers allow people to explore maps of the seas and oceans quickly and easily.

Chapter Five

Future of Sea Mapping

The first maps created with computer technology were weather maps made in 1950 with the help of the first electronic calculator. By the 1980s, smaller and more powerful desktop computers were used in producing the first electronic atlas, developed in Canada in 1982. By 1989, a digital map of the world was available on the MundoCart **CD-ROM**. This achievement made interaction with the map information used to compile modern maps much easier.

This man holds a GPS device in his hand. This device will help him always know his location while he operates a submersible.

Navigators today rely not only on high-technology tools such as computers and satellites, but also on the **Global Positioning System** (GPS) to find their longitude as well as latitude. Launched in 1978, GPS is a radio-based navigation system of twenty-four satellites in orbit around the Earth. They broadcast their exact time and position to ground-based receivers, from which navigators can accurately determine the time as well as their ship's position and speed. GPS units are now small enough to be attached to laptop computers or held in the palm of the hand.

Types of Sea Charts and Maps

Sea charts and maps help sailors to navigate. Besides sea charts and maps, there are many other kinds of charts and maps used in sea travel and research. Maps that show a considerable amount of detailed information about channels, harbors, currents, and water depths are called nautical charts. They are designed to help guide boats.

Bathymetric maps show the topography, or shape, of the bottom of a body of water such as a sea or ocean. Current and

A Little Help from Our Friends

Marine animals, such as turtles and manatees, are fitted with transmitters that relay information about their location. Satellites pick up the signals they give off, which provides mapmakers with environmental information, such as the depth, water temperature, or possible pollution of the waters in which the animal swims. Satellites that detect and observe characteristics and features of the seas and lands are called environmental satellites.

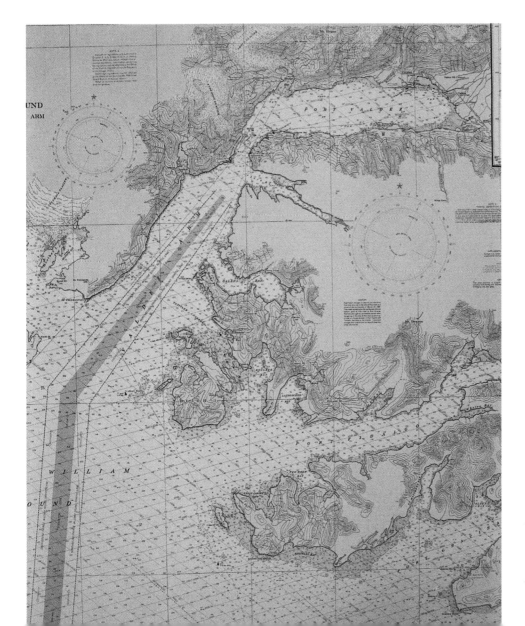

This chart helps people navigate through Prince William Sound.

tide charts provide information on those aspects of the seas. Water temperature charts give that information on a weekly, monthly, or annual basis.

Weather maps are special-purpose maps that record the weather over a given part of the world. They are of two types—climate maps and meteorological maps. Climate maps show the average or standard weather at a place over years or centuries. Meteorological maps show short-term weather patterns that last from a day to a few months.

Present and Future Sea Mapping

Oceanographers have built a new acoustic system for tracking temperature variations and currents. Others developed a buoy—a floating device—which collects surface current information and transmits it via satellite to Great Britain and France. Other new tools or technologies for sea research and mapping include a deep-towed sonar scanner for studying the oceans, computerized sea traffic control systems, and instruments for checking the cleanliness of coastal waters.

Another new technology for mapping the seas, the Global Sea Level Observing System (GLOSS) consists of a worldwide network of 287 stations that monitor long-term climate change and sea levels. Many of them use the latest technology to generate real-time measurements. They are relayed to a computer network via telephone systems or satellite. At the same time, another technology called satellite **altimetry** is providing sea-level data every ten days with a precision of within a few centimeters that is transferred to maps.

These and other technologies help predict global warming and sea-level rise. Global warming is a phenomenon in which the planet and its seas and oceans are gradually warming. This creates potentially very destructive atmospheric and weather changes and could speed up a rise in ocean levels that would threaten coastal cities.

Scientists monitor the sea level and temperature to watch for changes related to global warming.

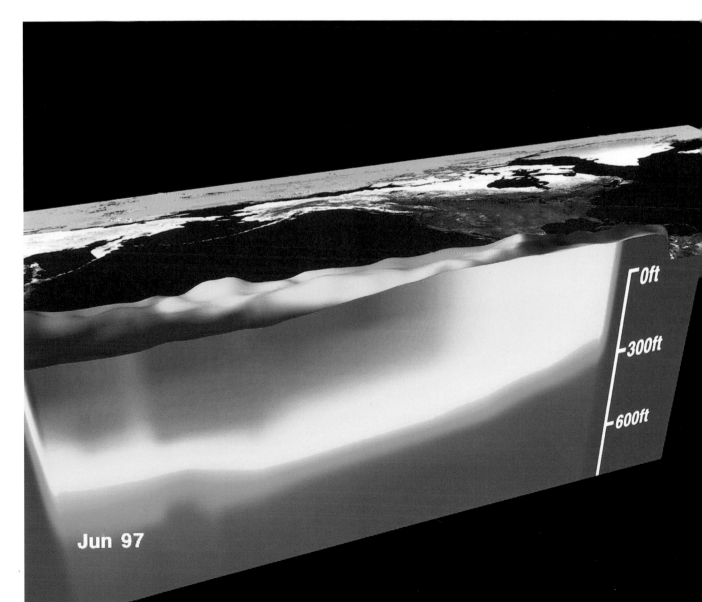

National Survey Plan

The National Oceanic and Atmospheric Administration (NOAA) is currently in the process of providing basic data, charts, and maps on the seas 200 miles (321.8 km) offshore from the nation's coastlines. Called the National Survey Plan, the extensive project will provide information for the safe navigation of the waters. Basic data will be collected for engineering, scientific, and other commercial and industrial activities. The surveys are to be of the oceans along the East and West Coasts, the inland Great Lakes, Alaska's coasts and waterways, the Gulf of Mexico, Puerto Rico and the Virgin Islands, and Hawaii and other Pacific islands.

The seas and oceans are the most complex, challenging, and harsh environment on Earth, and accessing it requires technology. It has only been within the last fifty years that technology has advanced to the point that the ocean is being examined in a systematic and scientific way. New technology for mapping the seas is evolving today and will continue into the future. Information acquired from the seas can have profound effect on the environment, the weather, and the extent and use of the planet's vast natural resources.

Future research and mapping can lead scientists to learn more about the abundant mineral supplies from the ocean floors. Renewable energy might be achieved from the moving sea, just as the Sun provides heat, and wind power produces energy to move machines. Medical drugs and other useful chemicals may be extracted from the vast biological wealth of the oceans, from plants and animals not yet discovered or studied for their potential benefit to mankind. New and as yet unknown food sources to feed the hungry of the world may still be discovered in the depths of the seas.

As many scientists studying the seas caution, on a global scale, what happens on land and in the sky affects the oceans. To know what is in the waters making up over 70 percent of the planet, and to map that knowledge, is essential because what happens to the oceans affects us all.

Timeline

B.C.

1500	Phoenicians sail the Mediterranean Sea. Polynesians begin to explore the Pacific Ocean.
700	Phoenicians sail around coast of Africa.
431	Maps are drawn for the Peloponnesian Wars.
300s	Greeks make globes. Maps are drawn for wars in the Mediterranean.

A.D.

100s	Greek Marinus of Tyre makes early sea charts.
150	Greek astronomer Ptolemy creates a set of books called *Geography*.
1200s	Portolan navigation charts of the Mediterranean Sea are drawn.
1300s	Ptolemy's world map is rediscovered in Europe.
1472	First map is produced on a printing press.
1500s	Gerardus Mercator charts the world's seas.
1507	Martin Waldseemüller publishes his *World Sea Maps*.
1513	Vasco Núñez de Balboa walks across Panama and sights the Pacific Ocean.
1521	Ferdinand Magellan's expedition completes the first circumnavigation of the Earth.
1690	Edmund Halley invents the diving bell.
1760s	John Harrison's chronometer makes it possible to determine accurate longitude.
1768–1779	Captain James Cook explores the Atlantic and Pacific Oceans.
1795	British Hydrographic Office is established to chart the seas.
1840s	U.S. Navy studies ocean currents and winds.

1870s	Expedition of British ship *Challenger* studies the seas.
1914–1918	Battle maps are drawn during World War I.
1937	Radar is invented.
1939–1945	Battle maps are drawn during World War II.
1950–1952	*Challenger II* makes precise soundings of ocean depths.
1957–1958	International Geophysical Year produces studies of seas and oceans.
1964	U.S. Navy's Sealab project is begun to study living underwater.
1965–1966	Various nations conduct study of the Atlantic Ocean.
1972	Landsat satellites are launched by the United States to aid in mapmaking from space.
1978	Global Positioning System begins, providing satellite surveying from orbit in space. Seasat-A satellite is launched to study world's oceans.
1982	Canada produces first electronic atlas.
1990s	Maps are drawn recording depths of the oceans.

Glossary

acoustic—related to sound or hearing

altimetry—measuring altitude

astronomer—a person who studies the stars, planets, and space

atlas—a book of maps

bathysphere—an underwater diving station

botanist—a person who studies plants

cartographer—a person who draws, plans, and studies maps

CD-ROM—stands for Compact Disk Read-Only Memory. It is a small laser-encoded optical disk that stores data.

chronometer—a clock that helps determine longitude

circumference—the distance around the rim or outer edge of a circle

circumnavigated—sailed around

compass—a navigational instrument for determining direction by showing where north is

continent—one of the seven large land masses on Earth

current—the movement of water in an ocean or river

diving bell—a bell-shaped vessel used to take people underwater

electromagnetic wave—a wave produced by the speed of an electric charge

equator—the imaginary line circling the Earth at latitude zero degrees. The starting point for measuring north and south on a map or globe.

Global Positioning System—a system whereby surveying information is beamed from satellites to receivers on Earth

globe—a sphere on which a map of the Earth or sky is depicted

latitude—how far a place is to the north and south of the equator

longitude—how far a place is to the east or west of the prime meridian

microwave—an electromagnetic wave that can pass through objects

navigator—a person in charge of or skilled in navigation

oceanographer—a scientist who studies the seas and oceans

oceanographic—related to the study of the seas and oceans

oceanography—the science of the seas and oceans

orbit—the path of an object circling a planet or the Sun

portolan chart—a medieval chart that helped sailors reach their destinations at sea

radar—a detecting device utilizing radio waves

satellite—an object in outer space that orbits Earth, other planets, or other celestial bodies

sonar—sound navigation ranging instruments that use sound to map the bottoms of seas

soundings—calculating the depths of bodies of water

submersible—a ship capable of operating underwater

surveillance—to watch someone or something closely

surveying—collecting information about the land by measuring its size and shape

trench—a long, narrow underwater valley

To Find Out More

Books

Black, Jeremy. *Maps and History*. New Haven, CT: Yale University Press, 1997.

Blandford, Percy W. *The New Explorer's Guide to Maps and Compasses*. Blue Ridge Summit, PA: Tab Books, 1992.

Borgese, Elisabeth Mann, editor. *Ocean Frontiers: Explorations by Oceanographers on Five Continents*. New York: Abrams, 1992.

Brewer, Paul. *Explorers and Exploration: Vol. 2: The Golden Age of Exploration*. Danbury, CT: Grolier, 1998.

Ganeri, Anita. *The Story of Maps and Navigation*. New York: Oxford University Press, 1997.

Harris, Nathaniel. *Explorers and Exploration: Vol. 1: The Earliest Explorers*. Danbury, CT: Grolier, 1998.

Johnson, Sylvia A. *Mapping the World*. New York: Atheneum, 1999.

Pratt, Paula Bryant. *Maps: Plotting Places on the Globe*. San Diego, CA: Lucent Books, 1995.

Organizations and Online Sites

Ancient History: Maps
http://ancienthistory.about.com
This online site provides a wealth of information on maps and geography of the ancient world.

History of Cartography
University of Minnesota
2221 University Avenue SE
Minneapolis, MN 55414
http://www.-map.lib.umn/history_of_cartography.html
The John R. Borchert map library at the University of Minnesota offers extensive information about maps throughout history.

National Imagery and Mapping Agency
http://164.214.2.59/nimahome.html
This government agency's online site offers maps of the sea and land as well as information.

National Oceanic and Atmospheric Administration
http://www.nnic.noaa.gov
Visitors to this site can access information, maps, and photographs from NOAA's Network Information Center.

Orsher Map Library
University of Southern Maine
Box 9301
Portland, ME 04104
http://www.usm.maine.edu/~maps/
The Orsher Map Library at the University of Southern Maine contains a wide range of online exhibits about maps of the past and present.

U.S. Geological Survey
http://www.usgs.gov
This government agency offers information on mapping and geology as well as educational resources in cartography through its online site.

A Note on Sources

I've always loved studying maps. When I was a boy growing up during World War II, I used to draw my own smaller-scale versions of full-page maps in the newspapers. Each day, they showed where the war was being fought in Europe, the Pacific, or Africa. I learned a great deal about world geography that way and developed a lifelong fascination with maps. I papered my college dormitory room with *National Geographic* maps, covering the ceiling as well as the walls.

When I research to write a book, I try to combine library research with contacting experts on the subject. In researching maps in history I had to rely primarily on libraries. I had the help of research librarians at four nearby libraries in Chicago, Evanston, Wilmette, and Glenview, Illinois. They recommended both adult and juvenile books on map history and I began by reading those for young readers, then graduated to the adult books. For young readers, I found the most helpful basic books on mapping the seas to be Nathaniel Harris's *The Earliest Explorers* and Paul Brewer's *The Golden Age of Exploration.*

I also sit at my computer and go online to surf the World Wide Web for sites to help me research a subject. For researching mapping the seas, the online sites I list in the To Find Out More section were especially helpful.

—*Walter Oleksy*

Index

Numbers in *italics* indicate illustrations.

About the Author

Walter Oleksy has been a freelance writer of books, mostly for young readers, for over twenty-five years. He came to that occupation after several years as a newspaper reporter for *The Chicago Tribune* and as editor of three feature and travel magazines. A native of Chicago, he received a bachelor of arts degree in journalism from Michigan State University, then was editor of a U.S. Army newspaper for two years before starting his writing career.

He lives in a Chicago suburb with his best friend Max, a mix of Labrador Retriever and German shepherd. They take frequent walks in the nearby woods and swim in Lake Michigan.

His most recent book for Children's Press is *The Philippines*. His other books for young readers include *Hispanic-American Scientists* and *American Military Leaders of World War II*.